THE FACEBOOK ADDICT'S SURVIVAL GUIDE

By Martin Baxendale

© Copyright Martin Baxendale 2011

Published by Silent But Deadly
Publications, 21 Bisley Road,
Stroud, Glos., GL5 1HF

Printed in England by
Stoate & Bishop Printers Ltd,
Shaftesbury Industrial Centre,
Cheltenham, Glos. GL51 9NH

ISBN: 978-0-9562398-3-9

CONTENTS

INTRODUCTION

If like me and my wife you're a Facebook addict, spending <u>far</u> too much time online chatting, updating your status, checking out other people's profiles, photos, pages etc, then you basically have two choices:

A) Try to kick the habit: Delete your account, stay off Facebook, go cold turkey and end up a nervous wreck constantly wondering what you're missing and desperate to get back on again and catch up.

B) Sneakily conceal your addiction and continue feeding your habit while craftily disguising the effects it has on your everyday life and hope that people don't notice that underneath the calm and collected exterior you're a Facebook-crazed junkie with a status-update monkey on your back.

I strongly recommend you choose **B)**. It's what my wife and I do. We were constantly yelling at each other to stop wasting so much time on Facebook, until we realised that just being sneaky and underhand about our Facebook addictions was so much easier.

A typical Facebook chat between me at my desk at home and my wife in her workplace.

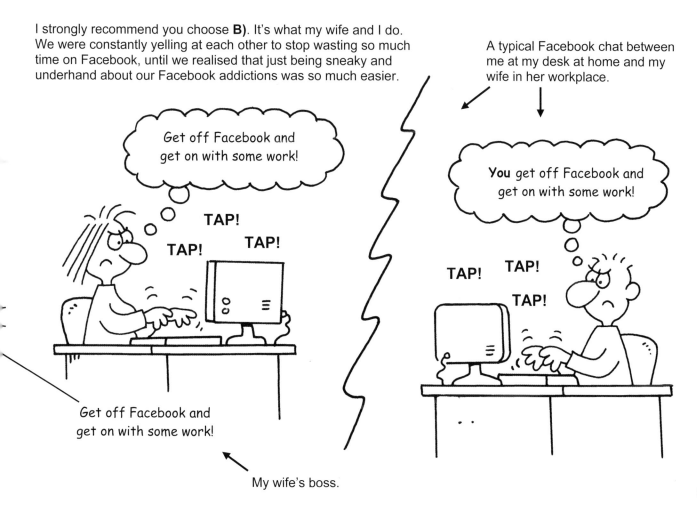

Get off Facebook and get on with some work!

TAP! TAP! TAP!

You get off Facebook and get on with some work!

TAP! TAP! TAP!

Get off Facebook and get on with some work!

My wife's boss.

If you do for some insane reason choose to try **A)**, kicking the habit, then it may help to form a local Facebook Addicts Anonymous group where you and other crazed Facebook junkies can help each other to go cold turkey and not backslide.

My wife and I tried this once, but unfortunately it didn't work out. What a shame, but at least we tried, eh?

Whose idea was it to hold our first meeting in an **internet café**?!

TAP!
TAP!
TAP!
TAP!
TAP!
TAP!
TAP!
TAP!
TAP!
TAP!
TAP!
TAP!
TAP!

FACEBOOK ADDICTS ANONYMOUS

MEETING HERE TODAY

HOW TO HIDE YOUR FACEBOOK ADDICTION

I can recommend this set-up, which I devised to help me hide the fact that I'm on Facebook all the time. It works equally well at home and in the workplace.

Mirror for checking behind you.

Pressure pads under carpet all around desk set off warning light when stepped on.

Infra-red motion sensors covering all approaches to your desk.

Sensitive heat-detectors set off warning light if they pick up even slight rise in air temperature from body heat of another person approaching your desk.

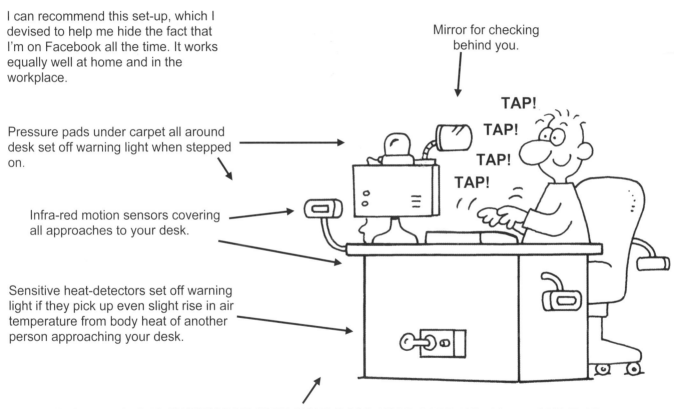

EARLY-WARNING SYSTEM PREVENTS YOUR BOSS, YOUR PARTNER, OR ANYONE ELSE SNEAKING UP ON YOU AND CATCHING YOU WASTING TIME ON FACEBOOK YET AGAIN.

And of course there are many other ways to hide your Facebook habit from those who think that you waste far too much time on it...

Status update: Hiding in the toilet with my laptop, pretending to have the runs! LOL!!!

Hurry up! You've been in there for **three hours**!

Sorry! I've got the **runs**! Oh, God! Will it never stop?!

TAP! TAP! TAP! TAP!

TOILET

SPLLRRRP!

SPLLRRRP!

SPLLRRRP!

Tape recording of custard being squirted into a bucket for simulated diarrhoea sound effects.

BURSTING!

JIGGLE! JIGGLE!

10

PREVENTING INTERRUPTIONS

Don't you just hate having your Facebooking interrupted by the annoying demands of other people, and other things that <u>have</u> to be done? Well there's stuff you can do to avoid that.

First, other people wanting you to get off the computer so they can use it, or just wanting to "help" you to cut down on the amount of time you waste on Facebook by endlessly nagging you to get off it.

Wrist handcuffed to laptop or keyboard.

Mouse duct-taped to hand, to stop anyone taking it away.

My dear wife duct-taped to chair, and chair chained to desk.

Will you **please** get off sodding Facebook for **five minutes**! I need to use the bloody computer!

GRRRRRRR! Don't come any closer! I'm warning you! **Stay back**!

I devised this set-up to minimise the number of times I have to interrupt my Facebooking and leave the computer to do other things. You could easily fix up something similar for yourself.

No I **wouldn't** like to discuss changing my f***ing electricity supplier, now **sod off**!

Hosepipe to toilet, so you don't have to stop Facebooking to go for a pee. Make sure you fit a stop-cock tap to stop any back-flow when you're not using the pipe, and especially to prevent pranks like the time my dear wife put the other end onto a cold tap and turned it on full blast "just for a laugh").

Intercom between desk and front door, to save having to answer the door to annoying, time-wasting callers.

You'll also need to fit a pump if the toilet is upstairs and your computer is downstairs. Make sure you don't fit the pump the wrong way round (that's a mistake I won't make twice!)

PSSSSSS!

YANK!

Plug-in hosepipe "Lady Wee" adaptor for female users.

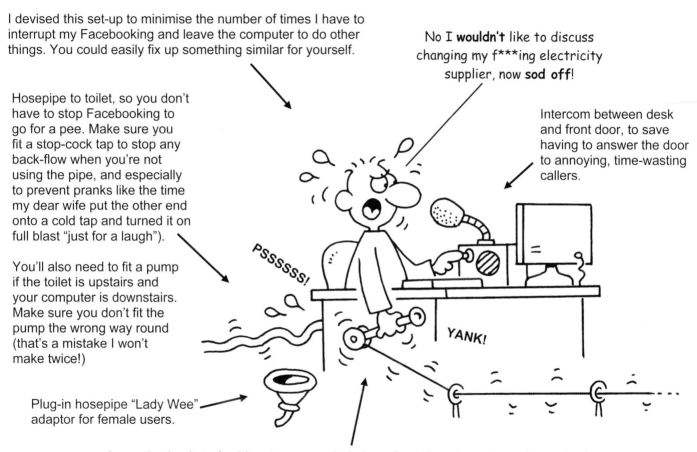

Lever tips bucket of cold water suspended above front door, to soak persistent doorbell ringers who won't go away (I don't care if they <u>have</u> forgotten their keys, they'll remember them next time, won't they! Oh and for Jehovah's Witnesses, just for the hell of it).

13

A conveyor-belt device like this from the kitchen to your computer desk will save you having to leave Facebook to get cups of coffee and tea, fetch snacks, eat meals etc.

Of course it rather depends on having someone at the other end who's prepared to keep loading it with food and drink for you. Yes, I know that's a bit of a design flaw, and yes in our case my dear wife does refuse point blank to have anything to do with it…except of course when <u>she</u>'s on Facebook. *

* Actually, she did just the once use this to send me a bowl of what I thought was cereal but which turned out to be used cat litter. I was so absorbed in Facebook that I ate half of it before I realised. You live and learn.

Dogs and cats can also be a serious distraction, constantly demanding that you tear yourself away from Facebook to see to their needs, and howling or meowing endlessly and irritatingly if you don't. Unless of course, like me, you make alternative arrangements...

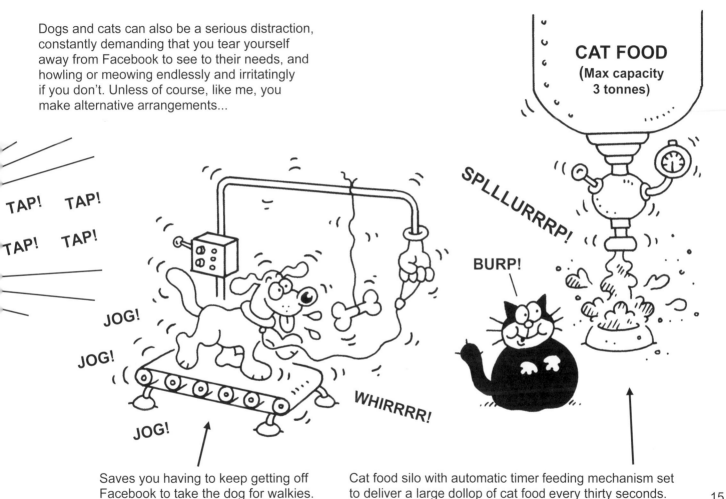

CAT FOOD
(Max capacity 3 tonnes)

TAP! TAP!
TAP! TAP!

JOG!

JOG!

JOG!

SPLLLURRRP!

BURP!

WHIRRRR!

Saves you having to keep getting off Facebook to take the dog for walkies.

Cat food silo with automatic timer feeding mechanism set to deliver a large dollop of cat food every thirty seconds.

15

HOW TO BE ON FACEBOOK WHILE DOING OTHER STUFF

Sometimes there's stuff you have to do that simply can't be done while sitting in front of your computer at a desk or table. But that doesn't have to mean logging off and missing out on valuable Facebook time.

With a little ingenuity you can stay on Facebook almost constantly, only logging off to sleep (and even then I have been known to set my alarm for the middle of the night just to check for insomniacs who might be up for a Facebook chat).

For example, I can strongly recommend the following stratagems, which have always worked well for me and my wife. Note: The devices illustrated will soon be available to buy from my new website www.facebookaddictessentials.com, or of course you can make them yourself with a few basic tools and everyday materials.

Status update: No more hot water and starting to go a bit wrinkly.

Battery-operated mini windscreen wiper for steamy, misted-up laptop screen.

Detachable inflatable laptop floats, held on by suckers.

Inflatable mouse pad.

Novelty rubber-duck mouse.

FACEBOOKING IN THE BATH

FACEBOOKING AT PARTIES

Of course you'll want to move around and socialise at parties, maybe even have a bit of a dance, and with this useful little laptop accessory you can do all that <u>and</u> still be on Facebook all the time.

Laptop docks neatly into the handy party carry-tray device, supported by inconspicuous shoulder straps.

Drinks glass holder attachment fixes to laptop with sucker.

Automatic hand-shaking attachment.

Plate holder attachment for nibbles, sandwiches, dips etc.

Using your phone in the cinema can make you very unpopular, let alone tapping away on your laptop keeping up with Facebook.

But no-one will tell you off if you're inside this baby. I originally made it so my dear wife wouldn't keep complaining and hitting me for eating my popcorn and slurping my drink so noisily ("like a sty full of pigs at feeding time" I think were the exact words she, and the people three rows behind us, used).

Anyway, I quickly realised it was also perfect for watching the film and still being on Facebook without annoying anyone else. You could easily construct something similar, but do remember to include some air holes. That was a design fault on my first prototype that only came to my attention after the paramedics resuscitated me at the end of the last Harry Potter film.

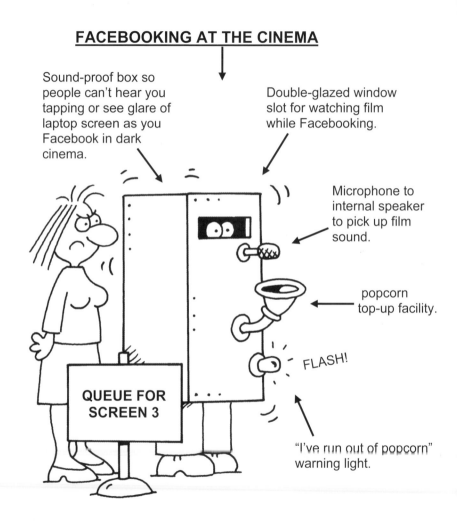

FACEBOOKING AT THE CINEMA

Sound-proof box so people can't hear you tapping or see glare of laptop screen as you Facebook in dark cinema.

Double-glazed window slot for watching film while Facebooking.

Microphone to internal speaker to pick up film sound.

popcorn top-up facility.

FLASH!

QUEUE FOR SCREEN 3

"I've run out of popcorn" warning light.

You can of course do a little discreet Facebooking on your mobile phone in some social situations without people noticing too much, but that's never as satisfying to the true addict as mainlining Facebook on a desktop computer or laptop.

When dining out, for example, nothing beats the old "Oops, I've dropped my fork" excuse to duck under the table for a quick bit of Facebook time on your laptop. Works for me every time.

FACEBOOKING IN RESTAURANTS

Oops, I've dropped my fork under the table. I'll just get it!

Oooh! I'm going to get some naughty under-the-table oral sex!

TAP! TAP! TAP! TAP! TAP! TAP! TAP!

At major social events, wedding ceremonies for example, Facebooking during the main event - even discreetly on a mobile phone - is distinctly frowned upon.

Not that such piffling social constraints would necessarily put off a truly hardened Facebook addict, and it certainly didn't prevent my own dear wife from taking a moment or two to update her Facebook profile. I just hope no-one noticed.

Relationship status: MARRIED.

TAP! TAP! TAP!

SNIFF! WIPE!

Of course there are <u>some</u> social occasions where being
discovered Facebooking during the proceedings wouldn't
just be frowned upon but would be truly shocking. But
possibly worth it to see the looks on people's faces.

Having your partner catch you going on Facebook while you're having <u>sex</u> with them can also prove highly embarrassing. So if you must do it, at least try not to get found out.

My dear wife was so sneaky about it that it was a long time before I realised just what was going on. It would probably be a lot more discreet to use a mobile phone but she doesn't do things by halves. Plus I don't think she really cared all that much whether I found out or not.

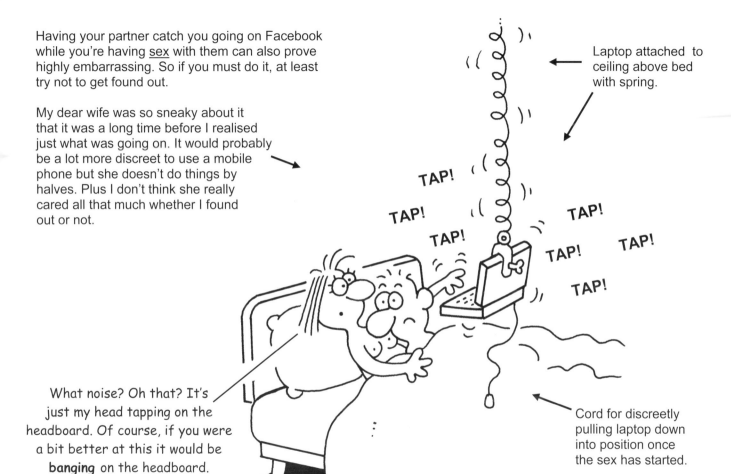

Laptop attached to ceiling above bed with spring.

TAP! TAP! TAP! TAP! TAP! TAP! TAP! TAP!

What noise? Oh that? It's just my head tapping on the headboard. Of course, if you were a bit better at this it would be **banging** on the headboard.

Cord for discreetly pulling laptop down into position once the sex has started.

Thinking back, all the signs were there but I just didn't see them. I sometimes wonder if there's ever been a time when we were having sex and she <u>wasn't</u> on Facebook.

24

25

Do you resent time wasted driving to and from work, to the supermarket, to visit friends and relatives, etc, etc, when you could be enjoying yourself on Facebook instead?

My wife, the ultimate hardcore Facebook addict, certainly did. But she came up with a very simple answer, which she insists I recommend to you.

Apparently all you have to do is drive backwards and forwards very fast past a speed camera until you get enough points for a long driving ban, then let some other mug (i.e. me) do all the driving while you relax and become a backseat driver and backseat Facebooker. →

Status update: We're lost and the sat nav's broken, but will he stop and ask for directions? Nooooooo! Of course not!

If you **must** be on your bloody laptop while I'm driving, you could at least go on Google Maps and try to work out where we sodding are!

TAP!
TAP!
TAP!
TAP!
TAP!

VROOOOM!

ENHANCING YOUR FACEBOOK EXPERIENCE

You can improve your Facebook experience in various ways.

For instance, changing your job to something more exciting might allow you to post much more eye-catching status updates that would get you far more attention on Facebook, attract more comments, get you more friends, etc. For example...

Our friend Brad, the airline pilot updating his Facebook status.

Status update: Brad is **crash-landing in the sea** with 300 passengers aboard his plane! Wait, no...Brad has started the engines again with a 15,000 ft. power-dive. Yay! :) :) :) :)

Comment: PHEW!!!!

TAP!

TAP! TAP!

✓RIGHT!

A good example of a job with lots of potential for very interesting Facebook status updates.

Footnote: Since this book was written, our friend Alfred the accountant realized that he needed a change of career to something with more scope for thrilling Facebook status updates. He is now a chartered surveyor.

In much the same way, some **hobbies** are far better for Facebook status updating than others, providing more interesting and exciting material for status updates or simply more frequent opportunities to change your status.

For example, our friend Jenny the bungee jumper has the perfect excuse to change her Facebook status a lot.

Compare that with our friend Percy the bonsai tree grower's far less frequent updates about **his** hobby.

See what we mean? Think about it. Do **you** need a more Facebook-friendly hobby?

Status update: Jenny is **up**. Status update: Jenny is **down**. Status update: Jenny is **up** again. Status update: Jenny is **down** again. Status update: Jenny is **up** again...

Status update: Since this time last year, Percy's bonsai tree has grown three millimetres. Watch this space for next year's update!

TAP! TAP!

TAP!

Block Percy... Remove Percy from friends...Report Percy for being boring.

YAWN!

29

It's also very easy to sex up your pictures on Facebook with the help of photoshop.

Putting up a pic of yourself walking the dog in the park? One quick photoshop session later and it's you walking the dog up Mt. Everest.

Think your profile photo isn't sexy enough? Crank up photoshop and you can superimpose the head of Brad Pitt or Angelina Jolie onto your body and instantly attract more Facebook friends than you could ever imagine or know what to do with.

The ultimate, of course, is to create a completely false, invented profile for yourself in which you're a rich, gorgeous jet-setter looking for someone equally desirable.

Just watch out that you don't end up falling for someone with an equally falsified and imaginary profile. That's what happened to me and my wife. She was "Glamorous filmstar and brewery heiress with huge tits and football season tickets" and I was "Johnny Depp lookalike with enormous willy and shares in a chocolate factory".

You can imagine the disappointment (and the throttling and punching) that ensued when we eventually met in the real world.

31

OTHER BOOKS BY MARTIN BAXENDALE

'THE SNOWDROP GARDEN' - Martin's first novel is a wickedly funny and heart-warming tale of love, misunderstandings and a last-ditch attempt to save one of England's most beautiful woodland snowdrop gardens from the builders' bulldozers. A really great, laugh-out-loud read.

'WHEN WILL MY BABY BRAIN FALL OUT?' - Martin's first children's book. Seven-year-old Millie struggles with her maths homework but then she gets hold of the idea that things will be better when her 'baby brain' falls out, just like a baby tooth, and her cleverer big-girl brain grows in its place. Should Mum and Dad put her straight or play along? A very funny yet charming story that will have children laughing out loud.

And some of Martin's best-selling cartoon gift-books:

'Your New Baby, An Owner's Manual' (over 500,000 copies sold).
'How To Be A Baby, An Instruction Manual For Newborns'
'Your Marriage, An Owner's Manual'
'How To Be Married, An Instruction Manual For Newlyweds'
'Life After 40, A Survival Guide For Women'
'Life After 40, A Survival Guide For Men'
'Life After 50, A Survival Guide For Women'
'Life After 50, A Survival Guide For Men'
'Martin Baxendale's Better Sex Guide'
'The Relationship Survival Guide'
'A Very Rude Book About Willies'
'The Cat Owner's Survival Guide'
'The Dog Owner's Survival Guide'
'Your Man, An Owner's Manual'
'Calm Down!! The Stress Survival Guide'
'Your Pregnancy, A Survival Guide'
'Women Are Wonderful, Men Are A Mess'
'The Garden Owner's Survival Guide'
'The Squirrel Murders'

These and other books by Martin Baxendale can be ordered from www.amazon.co.uk (search for Martin Baxendale, or search by title, in 'books') and from other online bookstores or any High Street bookshop.